W9-AFN-404

JAMES DEAN

MARCEAU DEVILLERS

JAMES DEAN

Translated from the French by
Jonathan Marks

Sidgwick & Jackson
LONDON

*There is no love of life without
despair of life.*
Albert Camus
(L'Envers et l'Endroit)

First published in Great Britain in 1987 by Sidgwick & Jackson Limited

Originally published in 1985 in France by Éditions Pygmalion/Gérard Watelet

First paperback edition January 1989

First reprint January 1989

Second reprint April 1990

Copyright © 1985 by Éditions Pygmalion/Gérard Watelet

Translation copyright © 1987 by Sidgwick & Jackson Limited

All rights reserved. No part of this book may be reproduced or
transmitted in any form or by any means, electronic or mechanical,
including photocopying, recording or by any information storage
and retrieval system, without permission in writing from the
Publisher.

ISBN 0–283–99811–3

Phototypeset by Falcon Graphic Art Ltd
Wallington, Surrey
Printed by Butler & Tanner Ltd
Frome and London
for Sidgwick & Jackson Limited
1 Tavistock Chambers
Bloomsbury Way
London WC1A 2SG

CONTENTS

DEATH OF A REBEL

This is James Dean. We are on a sound stage in Hollywood. Dean does not appear to be listening to his director. He is barely rehearsing and cannot stand still. He changes without notice the moves indicated in the script, the gestures and scenes which have been agreed, disconcerting his colleagues by the changes made to his responses, mumbling or chewing his words.

Then there is that playful look of his.

At the risk of disappointing his fans, I do not think that he died in his car — as did 50,000 other Americans during the same year — because he was desperate and tired of life, but more simply because he belonged to a generation — lost, mystified and indifferent.

His recklessness, the risks he took at the wheel, were the result of the climate of nonchalance, hollow and devoid of courage, in which he lived. Hence this solitude, not of the dilettante, but of the little boy lost.

On the previous day I had met Marilyn Monroe. She was bubbly and had the look of a sapphire and the freshness of dew. She was swathed in worsted and fur, yet she seemed to be naked, and unbearably without shame.

Everything sparkled around her, but this magical apotheosis had the scent of humility, abandonment, sharpness and anguish.

Much has been written about this heightened solitude in which the most adored stars take refuge, and which harms them and sometimes destroys them. Even in the silent era, a star would sink beneath the waves of the ocean and disappear out to sea.

8

Glory! But is this glory really the intoxication of money, the roar of the crowd, the sacrifices in the name of publicity, the endless strain, the constant tenterhooks, and living off one's nerves? Is it not rather the unbridled fear of watching a brilliant illusion disappear suddenly, which very often little or nothing can justify, but a fear which is nevertheless immeasurable.

In James Dean's presence, the same alarm bells sounded in me as with Marilyn Monroe. He, like her, tempted fate and sported death as entertainment.

All that either of them needed, he the 24-year-old gamin, she the 36-year-old woman, both imbued with the same anxiety, was a touch of fantasy, a true love affair, or a spark of adventure.

It is not desperation, but its rejection which invites lightning to strike.

It is extraordinary and mysterious that the sensation created by their deaths has not faded. From the dislocated corpse a radiant and sharp image bursts forth, as if in defiance of the laws of life and death, an image which nothing can erase.

The ceremony of this imperious appeal, the halo which surrounds the hero, and the fascination which it brings are magical realities. One is reminded of Cocteau when he spoke of Rimbaud:

'He has gone . . . but he will return.'

Maurice Bessy

JAMES DEAN

We cannot speak of cinema without mentioning the name of James Dean, the freshly plucked *fleur du mal*, James Dean, who *is* the cinema, in the same sense as Lilian Gish, Chaplin, Ingrid Bergman, etc.
FRANÇOIS TRUFFAUT,
February 1956.

It is now thirty years since François Truffaut asserted the greatness of this new actor. Since then James Dean has become the most mythical name in world cinema. The considerable cult which surrounded him remains without precedent in the history of the seventh art. The hero of a generation, he personified all the aspirations of youth, discovered a new audience and then became its hero. However, apart from these considerations which are not directly related to his art, James Dean remains above all the unique creator of a vibrant and poetic art, the epitome of all that is the adolescent world.

A world in an effigy

The cult, the myth and the legend of James Dean began with his funeral. The number of people who travelled to pay final homage to him exceeded the total population of Fairmount (2,872 inhabitants), the town of his birth, where the ceremony took place. The eulogy given by the Reverend Xen Harcey ended with these words: '. . . James Dean's career is not over, it is only beginning, and remember, God himself is directing the production.'

And so a whole generation of boys and girls under the age of twenty, emerged, claiming an effigy of their own, and they would want to know and understand everything about their hero.

James Byron Dean was born on 8 February 1931 in the small town of Fairmount, Indiana, at Green Gables Apartments on 4th Street (the birth certificate was registered at Marion town

Jimmy aged four

A childhood of rustic games . . .

. . .and of horses

hall) to Mildred Wilson, the daughter of Methodist farmers, and Winton Dean, a dental technician and a Quaker.

In 1936, the family settled in Los Angeles, close to the Hall of Justice, Winton having secured a post as a dental practitioner at Veterans' Hospital. Three years later, the young Jimmy lost his mother, who at the age of twenty-nine, died of lung cancer. The child was entrusted to his uncle and aunt, Marcus and Ortense Winslow and went to live on the 440-acre farm in Fairmount, with his cousins Markie and Joan, who were often referred to as his brother and sister. Before long he had immersed himself in a wide range of farming activities, such as horse riding, hunting, cattle rearing, and tractor driving.

In 1945 he started at Fairmount High School, where, despite third degree myopia for which he had to wear tinted spectacles, he was a member of the baseball and basketball teams for several years, and winner of the medal for best athlete. The pursuit of dangerous sports would, however, always be part of his life and trace the path of his career, which invariably wavered between art and sport.

After his father remarried, James Dean found himself a spiritual father in the person of the Reverend James de Weerd, a baptist minister and unorthodox churchman. An Epicure, fascinated by everything, he aroused in his protégé an interest in bullfighting, taught him to drive his Mercury, and accompanied him to grand prix and nurtured his taste for music, literature and philosophy.

Second from left, Jimmy in the school basketball team

By 1948 James Dean had developed a passion for racing cars, was playing the bongos, learning the clarinet and had discovered yoga and dramatic art. At this time his uncle bought him his first motorbike, a secondhand Triumph. Sporting blue jeans with leather knee patches, a black jacket and a red scarf, he did not go unnoticed in the small town of Fairmount.

On 21 June 1949, the Reverend entered his pupil for the Indiana State amateur dramatic art competition, held in Longmont. Dean performed an extract from Dickens' 'The Madman' for which he received a Pearl Statue and his first newspaper article in the *Marion Chronicle*. When term began again he enrolled as a law undergraduate at U.C.L.A., near Santa Monica. It was at this point that his father, with whom he was living, presented him with his first car, a secondhand M.G.

At college he became a physical education instructor and thought about being a basketball trainer, but after a few months was expelled from the faculty for punching two fellow students. He abandoned law without regret and took classes in dramatic art at U.C.L.A., and in 1950 he was noticed in the drama society production of *Goon With the Mind*, a play in which he drew an unusual and original caricature of Frankenstein.

In September of that year, the actor, James Whitmore took up the chair in dramatic art at U.C.L.A. For James Dean this was an important change, as Whitmore's teaching was anti-

School photo for the new school year . . .

. . . and first portrait

Jimmy, centre, with his baseball team

Jimmy at college

The first article about James Dean in the spring of 1949 in the Fairmount local paper

James Dean arrives in Manhattan in winter 1951-52

THE FAIRMOUNT NEWS

Volume LXXIV   Fairmount, Grant County, Indiana, Thursday, April 14, 1949   Number 12

F.H.S. Students Win State Meets

conformist, and very close to Strasberg's 'Method', in which he was greatly interested.

In the competition held at the end of the year, Dean insisted on taking on a role which was barely suited to his personality, that of Malcolm in *Macbeth*. The performance at the Royce Hall Auditorium was a flop and received generally unfavourable reviews. During the evening he made the acquaintance of the writer, William Bast, who introduced him into the world of socialites and intellectuals. At this time the Fairbanks Studios gave him his first important television role in a religious film, *Hill Number One*, in which he played John the Baptist. Then, through his friend, Richard Shannon's connections, he was cast in further roles in *Fixed Bayonets* and *Sailor Beware*, in which he gave intelligent performances. He was also given a small part in Douglas Sirk's *Has Anybody Seen My gal?*

Theatre and television in New York

On the advice of his teachers, James Dean decided to chance his luck in New York. He crossed the States by bus and arrived in Manhattan in the winter of 1951/52. He made his way to 44th Street and found the Iroquois Hotel, close to the Actors' Studio. He signed up at the Shure Agency, where impressario Jane Deacy found him spots as second and third voice-overs in advertisements for the television company CBS, and in May 1952 he was hired as the stunt-tester in the TV show *Beat the Clock*.

A rare photograph of James Dean attending a class at the Actors' Studio. He is in the first row (the third from left)

Despite his apprehension, he went along to the Actors' Studio where he was allowed to attend lectures. Later he was admitted as a full-time student. After his first performance and Strasberg's analysis, Dean decided that it was not to his liking and his ensuing entreaties on the subject to Jane Deacy have become legendary. After this, his links with the Actor's Studio dwindled to a few brief appearances.

On television he appeared in *Studio One, Danger, The U.S. Steel Hour, Cherokee Story*, and of some note *Death Is My Neighbour*, with Betsy Palmer, in which he played the part of a young man tortured by problems of a metaphysical nature. In September of the same year, he was hired as a member of the crew on a yacht owned by theatre producer Lem Ayers, who invited him to audition for the part of Wally Wilking in N. Richard Nash's play, *See the Jaguar*. Michael Gordon was directing, with Arthur Kennedy and Constance Ford in the lead roles. It appears that Kennedy had insisted on Dean being given the part. An *avant-garde* play, heavily laden with symbolism, Dean was locked in an ice house and tortured sadistically by Kennedy. *See the Jaguar* was staged in Connecticut, then in New York, where it met a frosty reception. After six perform-

Jimmy in his studio at 19, West 68th Street, New York

1951. First portrait of the actor by Joseph Abeles

Jimmy as Frankenstein, a curious and original caricature

James Dean in Gide's *The Immoralist*

ances the show closed, but James Dean was singled out for his performance. At the dress rehearsal, photographer Roy Schatt got to know him well and published a series of photographs with captions in *Life, Collier's* and *Red Book*. This initial recognition in New York theatrical circles was to bring him the stroke of luck he needed. The producer Billy Rose hired him to create the role of the homosexual Arab boy in *The Immoralist*, after the novel by Gide. The opening night took place in December 1953 at the Cort Theatre in New York, with Louis Jourdan and Geraldine Page as the leads, in a production by Daniel Mann. James Dean reached such heights of passion, nuance and complexity during his performance which was quite risqué for the time, that the David Blum Foundation awarded him the honour of 'Best New Actor of the Year'. He also received two other prizes: the Donaldson and Perry awards. It is well-known that Broadway critics have enormous influence over the careers of new actors, and their unanimous approval of Dean made it possible for Elia Kazan to send him to Hollywood with a seven year contract at Warner Bros. and to cast him as Cal Trask, the main character in *East of Eden*.

The Kazan Boy

Contrary to popular belief, James Dean was not a product of the 'Star System'. When *East of Eden* was released, his name was hardly known except among Hollywood professionals, who thought of him as a younger Marlon Brando. Gossip columnists and film journalists devoted little space to him, and when they did it was usually, and ironically, to the effect that a colony of young talents from the Kazan stable was waiting for its chance to walk in the footsteps of Marlon Brando and Montgomery Clift. They were nicknamed the 'Brando Boys' by some, the 'Kazan Boys' by others. The group had its hopefuls and its leaders: Paul Newman, Rod Steiger, Eli Wallach, and of course, James Dean. The 'Kazan Boys' found themselves in opposition to another group, the 'leading men', represented by actors such as Rock Hudson, Tony Curtis, Robert Wagner and Tab Hunter. According to informed opinion of the day, the 'Kazan Boys' cultivated a frenetic anti-conformism, which, in the eyes of some, were the latest mannerisms of a foolish

With the future president of the United States, Ronald Reagan, in *The Dark Hours*, December 1954

passing phase. The 'leading men', on the other hand, found favour with journalists on account of their amiable conservatism and their reassuring politeness.

The première of *East of Eden* was shown to an audience of 600 journalists, and made James Dean an overnight star; critics and others in the film world who had looked on him almost as an imposter surrendered to the evidence.

**6 May 1955,
his first television play,
with Pat Hardy in
*The Unlighted Road***

**3 December,
1952; Dean's first
appearance on the
Broadway stage in
See the Jaguar with
Arthur Kennedy**

The trilogy of the unloved one

The cinema had waited fifty years for an adolescent to claim his identity and parade it on the screen.

Before James Dean, except in a few rare cases, the adolescent was always portrayed as a psychological cypher. He was inferior, stupid, weak or ignorant, even cowardly or delinquent, and ultimately the 'foil' to the older generation. Even when the theatre threw up a sympathetic adolescent, he was almost always completely without charm or the power of seduction. With James Dean, the adolescent became a person in his own right. In this sense, *East of Eden* may be considered a turning point in the history of the cinema. The actor did not so much turn the 'awkward age' into a 'golden age', as take on 'the difficulty of being', which is adolescence, with its complexities, its uneasiness and uncertainties and make them traits worthy of the hero. By giving these characters an extraordinary power to communicate, Dean was to make cinematic history in his two short years of stardom from his performances in the roles of Caleb Trask (*East of Eden*), Jim Stark (*Rebel Without A Cause*) and Jett Rink (*Giant*). These three characters appear to develop chronologically from one film to the other with a certain psychological similarity in which the same emotions predominate, the complex of the 'unloved one' and its corollary 'the accursed son'. Dean's hero does not resemble traditional romantic heroes, he does not founder in despair or melancholy, he is not 'the sombre youth, the widower or the disconsolate one . . .' It is with the tenacious needs of the child, impudent, and sometimes awkward, even extravagant, that he struggles to claim the love of others. Rarely has an actor been able to inhabit the divide which separates the adolescent world from the adult world.

One 'Kazan Boy' pays another a visit. Brando, already
a veteran, comes to encourage the beginner James Dean (with Elia Kazan and Julie Harris)

A letter from James Dean to Barbara Glenn while he was appearing in *The Immoralist*

East of Eden is first and foremost a psychological study of the life of a seventeen-year-old boy who is roused from the somnolence of childhood. A spiritual orphan, his is the isolation of the struggle for love. James Dean enacts Cal's quest in a waking dream with the raw brushstrokes of a nightmare. This orphan state is to feature again, figuratively speaking, in *Rebel Without A Cause*, finally to find its voice in *Giant*. It is certain that James Dean found a mentor in Kazan, and Kazan never found another actor who fitted so well into his world.

The character of Cal was always thought to be James Dean's best performance and this stems from the depth of fevered nonchalance which he communicates to the audience. In a sense of profound identity he is Cal, Cal badly dressed (absence of his mother), hair wispy and wild (half asleep), shivering and huddled up (abandoned), he seems to be addressing himself to the audience beyond these great windswept solitudes. His heightened sensitivity pierces the screen, wanes, then waxes, expressing admirably the tormented quest for maternal and paternal love. Fits of fury, madness, seriousness, doubt, enthusiasm, laughter and tears, are all conveyed. *East of Eden* was shown at the Cannes Film Festival in April 1955, and although the public discovered James Dean with amazement, the critics greeted him cautiously. Some saw a questionable revelation in him, others stated quite categorically that he was a mediocre actor: '. . .The mystery of James Dean is the mystery of the void,' wrote Pierre Gaxotte for example. Fortunately, a young critic who was the same age as James Dean and soon to be instrumental in the 'new wave', recognized immediately in the deceased young man the actor for whom his generation had waited; Jean-Pierre Mocky, when asked for his opinin of James Dean, stated simply: 'James Dean, I think, was a truly important figure.'

François Truffaut, who the day after the film's release in France, wrote the review for the French cinema jounral *Cahiers du Cinéma*, had this to say:

The isolation of the fight for love.
James Dean and Julie Harris in *East of Eden*

A character awakened from the somnolence of childhood

The drama of the unloved one, *East of Eden*

. . . *East of Eden* is the first film to give us a Baudelairean hero, fascinated by vice and honour, who can embody both love and hate at the same time . . . James Dean has succeeded in making commercial a film which was scarcely so, in bringing to life an abstraction, and in arousing the interest of a huge audience in moral problems dealt with in an unusual manner . . . His myopic gaze prevents him from smiling, and the smile which can be drawn out of him with patience is a victory. His power of seduction is such — you

The quest for his mother

should have heard the audience's reaction when Raymond Massey refuses the money which equals love — that he could kill both his mother and father on the screen every night with the blessing of art-cinema audiences and popular audiences alike. His character in the film is a synthesis of *Les Enfants Terribles*, a solitary heir to the triple heritage of Elisabeth, Paul and Dargelos.
(Les Haricots du mal, *Cahiers du Cinéma*, No. 56, February 1956).

Roman Polanski, then a director in Poland, spoke of 'Kazan's wonderful *East of Eden*' and mentioned the names of Cybulski and James Dean among his favourite actors.
And finally this recollection by Georges Beaume:

. . .the first appearance of James Dean in *East of Eden* called to mind the first time we see S. Reggiani in *Le Carrefour des enfants perdus*, Gérard Philipe in *Le Diable au Corps*, Montgomery Clift in *The Heiress*, or Marlon Brando in *A Streetcar Named Desire*. He immediately joined the ranks of the very best. Standing out against them, however, with that mysterious gaze with which he would always look at his fellow actors without seeing them; the sudden tensing of the face which reeled from one emotion to another like a sinking ship; the laughter of the madman, the smart *roué*, which would tear at our heartstrings.

. . . An unusual look . . .

25

Rebel Without A Cause

The only hero of Greek tragedy in the cinema

Rebel Without A Cause will remain a masterpiece, because it is the American cinema's only Greek tragedy.

WILLIAM FAULKNER

The genesis of *Rebel Without A Cause* was of great significance, wrote André S. Labarthe in an analysis of the work: 'Everything begins, according to Nicholas Ray, both with innerbidden conviction and a pile of press cuttings. That is to say that the story of this film is at the same time the history of its author and the expression of a moment of the social history of the United States. How this "something important" became "the problems of kids growing up", how one night Nicholas Ray wrote a first sketch, "Blind Run" which told the story of three adolescents in a town in California, all this is the secret of this genesis.

'The seriousness with which Nicholas Ray planned to make this film meant that he would have to research the subject with psychiatrists, magistrates and specialists in juvenile delinquency. He consulted press cuttings from which he formed an impressive file. He surrounded himself with experts, or at least those who could shed some light on the problem. Leon Uris, the first scriptwriter he approached, "began by spending ten days as a trainee social worker at juvenile courts". Irving Shulman, the second, had been a high school teacher. Only the latter appeared on the credits beside Stewart Stern, who was responsible for the final script. "Blind Run", the first disjointed draft, became, as a result of the work of these three men, *Rebel Without A Cause*.

'The tautness of the script is to a great extent due to the tautness of its construction. Five parts, with the famous "chickie run" as the climax gives the work the tragic tone which its creator wanted. "Try to follow the classical form of tragedy," he remarked one day during its gestation period.'

Within the classic form of tragedy, we find the very principle of the three unities: time (the action takes place over a period of 24 hours, beginning on Easter night and ending the next day at dawn), place (Jim's family home, the university, the abandoned villa and its environs), action (imposed by the antagonis-

26

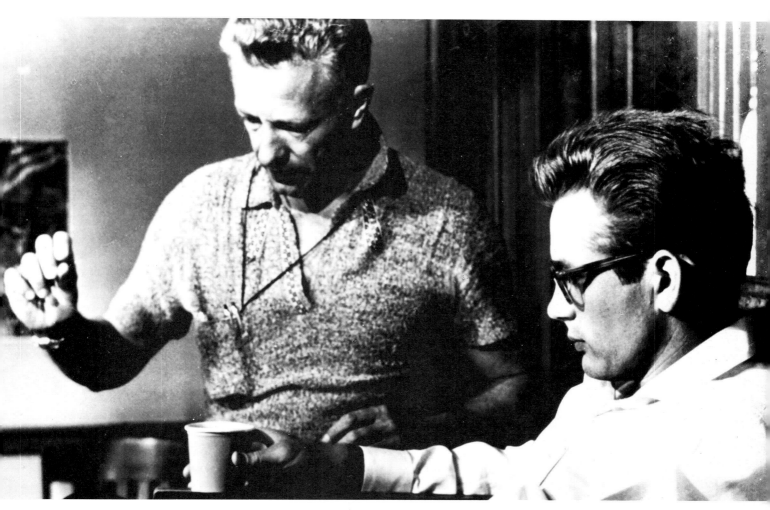

True friendship: Nicholas Ray directing James Dean

tic forces against which Jim must fight alone: parents, police, Buzz and his gang). From the baroque scenery of the landed bourgeoisie of Salinas Valley in 1917, we are launched in to a Cistercian style which constitutes the surrounding structure of *Rebel*, an ultra-modern university town, a very comfortably off family in the town, a solid line, but with dominant, almost fiery colours. Within this, the character of Jim Stark, consummate hero of pure tragedy and consequently the exact opposite of the little farmer with the sickened nonchalance in *East of Eden*, Jim Stark has short hair, the classical haircut, sober and elegant dress, sporting look, his physical aspect is proof of perfect equilibrium.

Of the three Dean heroes, Jim Stark can be represented symbolically as the central support of a set of scales, solid, upright and accurate, on which Cal tips upwards on the left and

27

Natalie Wood, script in hand, listens attentively to advice which the director gives to his leading man

With his Siamese cat, Marcus, a present from Elizabeth Taylor

Jett, downwards on the right.

Cal, because of his passionate torment, feverish entreaties, and desperate gestures, achieves paternal and maternal love in Abram. Jett would depend on abstract values: honour, wealth, power and vanity. To quench his thirst for love, he would only achieve a sense of pity and drown in nothingness. Jim Stark is a Corneillean hero in heroic destiny, he must fight alone, but also takes charge of others. Plato, in turn, commands affection and protection, Judy finds refuge in his arms. Even Buzz can only show him respect: 'I'm beginning to like you,' he tells him, some minutes before the 'chickie run' and it is likely that if the latter had not died, he would have demanded that Jim become leader of his gang.

Tab Hunter visits James Dean on the set of *Rebel Without A Cause*

The power of the myth across time: 30 years after his death, this image is still used to sell a brand of whisky

From the beginning of the film the hero appears threatened; his fate is also that of his generation, despite some measure of self control, his face betrays a worried smile. 'A boy wants to become a man, quickly. The problem is to show, during the course of this day, how he starts to become one.' But Jim does not want to become an adult, he is already one, and it is the adult world which he considers to be childish. Jim Stark wants to become a man in the noblest sense of the word, in other words to achieve dignity and self respect. '. . . Ray's heroes are lucid when they are trying to flee, they seek to unidentify themselves, destroying for a moment this society and the unacceptable reality which it confers on them.'

Rebel Without A Cause is the tragedy of an attempt to rebel and break free form the parental world, with a moment of escape into the dream world which is represented by the abandoned villa scene: 'Jim must face the gang, his parents, the police, and the universe, he is imprisoned by so many circles, from which he escapes one at a time. . . Jim, on his journey, passes through these circles, "the mirrors", and ends in the final maelstrom. The unleashing of passions and the rebellion of the heart were played out for the most part under the cover of night. He revolts against the inadequacy of the society in which he does not find the honour and purity of his generation'.

Jim Stark is much closer to Rodrigue than to one of the bikers in *The Wild One*. Should he respond to Buzz's challenge or fail in his duty and be thought of as a 'chicken', 'from both standpoints his troubles are without end'. When night falls, Jim, before facing the agonizing test, puts on his knights armour once again, in the form of a red nylon jacket and blue jeans.

31

A POSSIBLE FORM OF SPACE STATION

Jim Stark or the new world-weariness

Because the film was made while the phenomenon of the 'black leather jacket brigade' was gripping the imagination of journalists, there were those who insisted on labelling *Rebel Without A Cause* and its hero as representatives of this genre, and Nicholas Ray felt duty bound to protest since Dean did not wear a black leather jacket at any point in the film.

Between shots in *Rebel Without A Cause*, Jimmy affectionately dedicates his jacket to his friend Natalie Wood

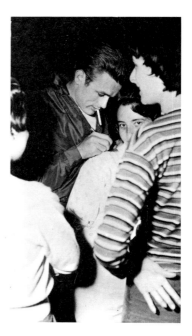

Extras, not wanting to miss out, ask for autographs

Rebel Without A Cause

It goes without saying that people didn't hesitate to accuse the film of influencing youth. In 1961, Nicholas Ray said, 'They reproached the film for creating the phenomenon, and in magnifying the characters and in particular the one played by James Dean, for having incited young people to imitate them. It's ridiculous, for a film can only reflect its time and keep pace with it. It can neither create it nor anticipate it. The phenomenon already existed: I was able to witness it both in Paris and in London, well before we started shooting the film, but it was ignored. The film unearthed it in full. And then of course there was that extraordinary portrayal by James Dean.'

Some critics were shocked by the character of Inspector Ray, who was shown in an idealized light, full of good intentions towards Jim. The Inspector, in charge of the juvenile delinquency service, is merely the exception which proves the rule, which renders him totally impotent. When Jim wants to see him, he is not there and Jim will be told so with hostility and indifference. He is also impotent when his colleagues kill Plato.

Meeting Plato (Sal Mineo)

Inspector Ray is really the alarmed conscience of Nicholas Ray which the latter projects into the character, hence the homonym, which is not in the least bit coincidental.

In time, the shower of prejudice heaped on this the latest reflection of world weariness has vanished as far as the film is concerned, and if we were to watch *Rebel Without A Cause* today, Jim Stark would seem to us to be an exemplary young man with both spirit and nobleness. Buzz's gang is no more than the manifestation of the symbolic danger threatening Jim, and recalls, in the same poetic manner, the Bacchantes of Saint-German-des-Prés threatening Orpheus.

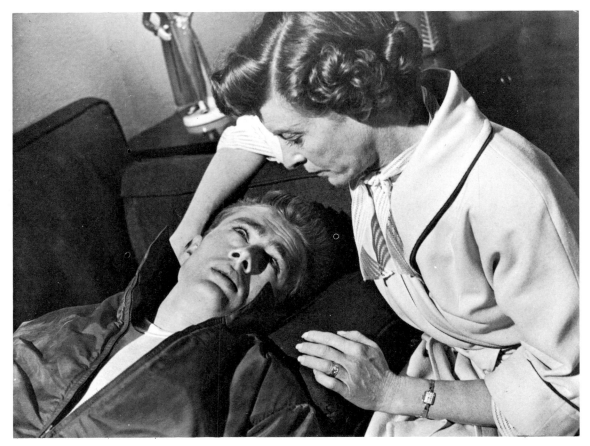

With Ann Doran

With Natalie Wood

It should be pointed out that the intrinsic fascination of *Rebel* is due to the disquieting conjunction of the conditions of death and the actor and his role, surrounding the work and its hero with a magic halo which might lead one to believe that the film had been made after his death. *Rebel Without A Cause* is also to a large extent the basis of the James Dean myth and left a deep impression on the press as a whole. Jean-Luc Godard wrote at the time:

. . . it is with this last film alone that Nicholas Ray finally seems to have made his mark both in the eyes of international critics and in the eyes of movie moguls . . . When he is not finding himself through them, he likes to make his actors play out their own characters, the recent example of James Dean, killed in a car accident at the wheel of the Porsche which he had just bought, is the greatest proof of all, and could easily be the epilogue to *Rebel Without A Cause.*

37

Jim and Inspector Ray (Edward Platt)

'*Rebel Without A Cause* took on a further dimension, as death had fixed for ever in the hearts and minds James Dean's incarnation of it. Jimmy, in any case, was "marked": he wanted to take on the most dangerous and tragic aspirations of our time!' (Nicholas Ray, *Cinémonde*, 11 April 1961).

39

Jimmy riding around on a mini-cycle in the Warner Studios

42

Giant

*'That's me, that's me because I convince myself
that it will be me, really me.'*★

When *Giant* was released the name James Dean, his two
previous films and his legend spread across the world. The
film, billed as a huge fresco of Texas, in the mould of *Gone
With The Wind*, turned out to be an unwieldy and rambling
film, and a great disappointment. According to the principles
of the genre, each big sequence opened and closed with
panoramic sweeps, the epic tone of which portends a wealth of
action. Between these shots, the epic is reduced to various
small domestic scenes, reserved and anodyne, between
Elizabeth Taylor and Rock Hudson at the turning point of the
three most important stages of their lives. In addition, a sense
of the 'popularity seeking' emanates from the work in which
bad taste often vies with it to the point of vapidness. However,
it was James Dean, more than any one, who was the focus of
this unanimous disappointment. Nevertheless, despite the
many reservations one might have about this, his final creation,
he remains the most captivating character in the film, and it is
certainly to him that *Giant* owes its stature.

It is fortunate that Alan Ladd turned down the role, for
Dean made Jett Rink into one of the most ambiguous figures of
all, outwardly horribly confused from crushing frustration, an
unhealthy awkwardness; internally eaten up with resentment
and puerile vanity. Dean inflates his creation right up to the
final fall, in tandem with the social rise of the character: he
moves from deceitful to underhand, and underhand to cowardly, from cowardly to vile. Before collapsing blind drunk, Jett,
almost unaudibly, gives away the secret of the untamed passion
which has controlled his life: his desperate love for Leslie
Benedict (Elizabeth Taylor) who can only show a sense of
maternal indulgence towards him. It is at this point that scorn
takes the place of pity, towards one of life's victims. James
Dean's stamp, in the first part of the film, is much greater than
one might believe, and as a result the influence of this role
would often be felt afterwards. In spite of his rare appearances

★ James Dean wrote this on the script of *Giant*, above the name of Jett Rink.

His fellow actor and friend, Liz Taylor

44

45

(barely twenty minutes in a film lasting over three hours, one cannot forget the way he inappropriately offers to shake Leslie's hand, his shuffling gait revealing the wretched aspect of his character, the way he paces his land, the tea given to Leslie in his cabin, where his hands no longer know what to do with the cup. In spite of this, the fact remains that the film leaves the public and fans of James Dean unsatiated. Dean's style is out of step with that of his fellow actors, who are as traditional as can be, and one can detect in him a retreat, a weakness which has re-entered his acting. Dean is no longer supported by the homogeneous nature of the casts of his two previous films, which on the one hand reinforces his marginal character of a young pariah, and on the other hand detracts from the unity of the film, and hinders considerably a psychological understanding of Jett Rink. He is completely detached from the whole and seems to be an almost superfluous addition, and this last impression is not without foundation since in Edna Ferber's novel the character of Jett is practically a non-entity; the adapters this time lacked boldness *vis-à-vis* the author is not developing Dean's role further. Finally, the portrayal of Jett Rink, as a fifty-year-old in the second half of *Giant*, caused doubt amongst critics, who brought his talent into question, often saying that he mercifully died at the right time. Dean could not effect this change in age, a change which the cinema can only achieve, even in the best of cases, in a manner which is always very approximate. However conscientious our young actor was in touching up his temples, whitening his hair, wearing a moustache and black heavy spectacles, it was all in vain: the morphology if his face was resistant to ageing, and through the close-fitting smoking jacket, a youthful body was visible which defied the passage of years. Besides, James Dean was not an epic actor; it was not that he did not become part of an epic, the photos taken of his work in *Giant* prove the contrary, but he did not express himself in it. James Dean was an intimist actor with an immediate need to confide,

With George Stevens

A now historic shot

Preparing for Giant with George Stevens

and above all a need for an equally intimate relationship with his director.

It has often been said that James Dean did not get along well with George Stevens, 'That the latter did not greatly appreciate James Dean's "flayed alive" style of acting, and Dean Steven's reproaches;' several weeks after James Dean's death, George Stevens wrote a thoughtful piece for *Modern Screen* which appeared to prove the contrary.

Strange wrong notes

In another statement, George Stevens asserted more expansively his appreciation for James Dean's work.

In France, the critics were on the whole divided about *Giant*.

'James Dean, quite curiously, throws strange wrong notes into this concerto of images and emotions, arranged too skilfully. His style of acting is the very antithesis of the sober and well-controlled acting of the other actors in the film.' (Louis Marcorelles, *Cahiers du Cinéma* 1957).

'In *Giant*, James Dean fascinates with his subtlety and "presence".' (Jean-Francis Held, *Ciné-Révélation*, March 1957).

'James Dean shows himself in his best light in the first part of *Giant*, but in his worst in the second. To play a fifty year old, he had to try and achieve a compromise, and descended to the level of third rate acting. The excessiveness of his performance would have been worse if the director had not for most of the time filmed his disarticulated puppet-like silhouette from the distance.' (Georges Sadoul, *Les Lettres Françaises*, 21 March 1957).

At the end of this triptych, of which the final panel closes on a ruined life, many wanted to see in it the premature testament of James Dean, which his death had suddenly laid uncovered. The fact remains that Dean preferred this role to the other more flattering and outstanding ones. He had become a public idol, but the question remains as to whether this stardom would have made a monster of him, a vain poseur, spoilt by such success in so short a space of time. Was he already aware of certain symptoms within which would betray his ideal of youth? This is surely a matter for consideration.

Today, James Dean's three films have become classics, but the new generation has reservations about these works; they lack real clout, and social and political issues, eroticism, and sexuality are completely absent.

We should side in the end with him: James Dean was not the twenty-year-old boy who took on the problems of his time, neither was he a pragmatic hero, a revolutionary, or even a rebel. James Dean expressed the ephemeral and complex crises of early adolescence of which the boundary is as loose as the last undefined flowering of childhood.

As a fifty year old . . . an age he would never reach

50

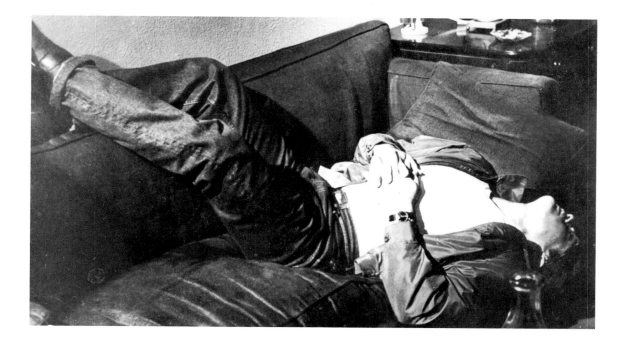

Portrait of an adolescent, by Joseph Abeles

James Dean and objects

The observer can take action – and that is all,
the object will always deny him its sense – and
its being.

J.-P. SARTRE

The credits of *Rebel Without A Cause* are superimposed directly
on the film's opening scene. James Dean, lying flat on his
stomach on the ground, stretched out at full length right up to
the edges of the cinemascope screen, plays with and watches a
little clockwork monkey. In this scene where he is drunk, he is
able to fill his conversation with the magical toy with wondrous
emotivity. This almost symbolic opening sequence reveals one
of the most original and richest aspects of James Dean's talent,
that of his sensorial relationship with objects. Rarely have we
seen an actor who could apprehend objects with the amazing
agility of an animal and give us what Antonin Artaud advo-
cated, in asking the actor to be foremost 'an athlete of the heart'
practising 'affective athleticism' within a unity of acting. This
feline quality of the body and limbs is without doubt the most
personal characterization, if not the very essence of James
Dean's acting, and if we had to try and confine *Rebel Without A
Cause* and *East of Eden* to their main performer, we should say
that he was the most progressive statement on modern art and
the actor's creation in the cinema.

Experimenting with the lasso

52

In 1956 Georges Beaume wrote: 'James Dean rubbing a bottle of cold milk slowly and interminably against his fevered face is for me an image which is inseperable from that scene in *Queen Christina* where we see Garbo caress the bed posts with her enamoured cheek . . .' This evocation of 'la Divine' when applied to James Dean might seem paradoxical and inappropriate, but it is however one of the most fitting, as the young actor possessed the same sensual powers as his famous elder, those of making poetry of what was around him and recreating a world from his personality alone. In this fight for expression, James Dean's physique always gained the upper hand, he used his entire body and it could speak, always unpredictably. The look is never where one might expect it, and the same can be said of attitude, movement or gesture.

A cord in his hands becomes an ironically sadistic object. Who could not be struck by the painful candour in front of Plato's corpse, where James Dean crouching, his face strained

Brando in *On the Waterfront*, directed by Elia Kazan

with tears, acts with his hands to try and overcome this unpleasant confrontation with death, an act which is inherent to beasts and children. We should remember how much the purpose of the most familiar objects can change when in his presence, as a skilfully used pullover serves as a shelter, bed and heating, a merry-go-round becomes a piece of gymnastic equipment, a red nylon jacket a shroud. At every moment, small touches of detail are introduced: there is not a single shot which does not show Dean taking stock, with an almost lucid instinct, of all that surrounds him. His senses experiment, utilize, combine and play with everything and nothing.

The least that one can say is that the collaboration of an actor like James Dean with his directors cannot be compared to that of choreographer and his dancer, and the genius of movement like that of gesture cannot be inculcated. We have spoken of nature, exhibitionism and superficiality, but it is a matter of style, James Dean's acting opens up a physical and expressive aesthetic of his personality.

François Truffaut, in his time, was one of the few critics to grasp the brilliance of the actor: 'His acting goes against fifty years of film-making. Each gesture, each attitude, each mime is

55

Montgomery Clift

A forerunner of the Actors' Studio style: John Garfield

a slap in the face of tradition. James Dean does not "show off" the script by using understatement, as does Edwige Feuillère, he does not poeticize as does Gérard Philipe. He is not anxious to show that he understands perfectly what he is saying. He acts beyond what he is saying and he always shifts the expression and the thing expressed. James Dean's acting is more animal than human. This is what makes it unpredictable. He can begin to turn his back to the camera whilst speaking, throw his head back or roll it forwards, he can raise his arms or push them forward. He belongs to those who pay no heed to rules and laws.'

James Dean and words

The emotion aroused by James Dean's creations sometimes caused people to hail a miracle, but any analysis of the genius of the child of a generation will always end up wedged between Elia Kazan and Marlon Brando. We should not forget that Montgomery Clift and John Garfield had, well before Brando, also used the Stanislavsky Method when working with Elia Kazan, hence the same sense of family among the four actors, but much more than belonging to a school, there are particular characteristic and physical analogies relating to these very definite aspects, which have today come to represent an incomparable breed of actors. This group characterized its time, both morally and physically, and its heroes have become to some extent the tragic characters of a social fatality of American history from Roosevelt to the end of McCarthyism. Beyond this similarity, if James Dean's influence became more intense than that of his predecessors, it is because he was their logical conclusion, taking the sensitivity of a style of behaviour to its limits. There are epic actors and intimist actors and in this case this is one of the major differences between Brando and Dean. As he belonged to both categories, Brando could easily change from quasi taciturn in *Viva Zapata* to the verbal deluge of *Julius Caesar*, even though the link between the two actors, based in part on the rejection of elaborate dialogue, the refusal of precise words and perfect diction, became a misunderstanding in the true sense of the word.

With Rock Hudson in *Giant*

Brando surprised the audience with his new manner of speaking, a single word, mumbled, the difficulty of enunciation, was prolonged by a series of looks and facial movements. The words were mumbled shyly in association with a particular gesture, which enriched the word behind the gesture and the gesture behind the word. The principal cause of this interpretation is to be found in the fact that Brando's characters were intellectually underdeveloped and even illiterate (*On The Waterfront, The Wild One, Viva Zapata*). Conversely, James Dean's characters, be it Cal in *East of Eden* or Jim in *Rebel Without A Cause*, were educated young men with money who had a proper mastery of the language. The word should be perceived without difficulty, but as much as Brando sought it, Dean rejected it. With Dean, an instinctive modesty demanded by the age of his heroes, always made the gesture precede the word, unless the latter was completely abolished. In *East of Eden*, when Julie Harris points out to him a Mexican woman employee and asks him whether he has made any advances to her and if so what kind, he replies with his eyes and little smiles. When his father refuses the money, not one word crosses Cal's lips, but instead a painful wailing crescendo.

Before hitting his brother Aron, the fit of rage is unleashed by one word bellowed with such force that it is deformed into a wild scream. On two occasions in *Giant* he gently rubs the palm of his hand thereby achieving a gestural antiphrasis to show

57

James Dean's acting
is always based on
an expression . . .

Rock Hudson ironically that all is well, whilst the latter becomes the deceived deceiver. In *East of Eden*, when he confides in Julie Harris (Abram) his desperation after attacking his brother Aron so savagely, lost in despairing thought, he allows the weight of his head to fall so brutally against the pillar of the balcony that his partner contorts in pain. These acts of mortification surface again in *Rebel Without A Cause* (the office of the commissioner beaten up in rage): we should see this not as a masochistic need (as with Brando), but as the desperate manifestation of rebellion against himself for acts committted which the juvenile conscience rejects. With James Dean, it is the physical which always has the last word.

. . . a physical
expression of his
personality

Poses . . .

Gestures and attitudes

The star can be thought of as a personality responsible for a character with its specific world. Two types of character can be identified: the monolothic (John Wayne, Charlton Heston) and the complex (Humphrey Bogart, Brando). The first, being attractive to a large audience which appreciate them passively, rarely prompt any unforgettable memories, nothing more than unconditional admiration, which is precisely the fate of the latter group. The complex characters, who are much more 'lived in', have in their possession a wide range of attitudes and expressions which arouse active and passionate feelings in the audience to the point of emulation. In this category, James Dean is the most consummate example. Dean was not an idol in his lifetime, and this sheltered him from affectation and from being the rallying cry for teenagers. James Dean's attitudes form an integral part of his acting style and the sporting disciplines to which he submitted are immediately obvious: yoga, dance and bullfighting form the basis of this physical expressiveness. For him this is a truly spiritual

60

exercise, and thus he makes punctuation marks from the poses which he strikes, and dialogues of the heart from his movements, the postures and furtive positions of his own physical language being physical metaphors as well.

It is in classic scenes such as the merry-go-round sequence in *East of Eden*, where Cal kisses Abram for the first time that Dean is at his best. When their lips meet, Dean leaves his arms outstretched and fingers spread, as though he were undergoing a delicate operation. This attitude, which eternalizes this first

and attitudes

61

Souvenir photo with the gang from *Rebel Without A Cause*

Dandy and casual in jeans

A completely different look

kiss, automatically diverts the viewer's eyes from Cal's lips to his hands, safeguarding all the modesty which the scene requires. It is such attitudes, which owe nothing to the *mise en scène*, which confirm a poet's sensitivity.

Orchestrating this sensitivity with all his being, the face is as active as the limbs, and what some took to be tics were in fact the writer's words. Where an actor uses his face continuously as a means of expression, a grin becomes a trace of humour, a slight cough a comma, an awkwardness is expressed by rubbing the nostrils, a defeat in a flexing of the body, the most fleeting of problems of existence in a muscular movement. To make this being live with intensity, such was his irrepressible vocation. In the phalanx of the Actors' Studio movement from which he had sprung, James Dean was to open up unexpected perspectives to actors and directors alike, for Dean was an actor who was in complicity with cinemascope and who was to contribute to a great extent to the acceptability of this format (which was still highly controversial at the time). Was he aware of this? Whether it was intuition of circumstance, the feeling is that his total allegiance to this format was responsible for his attitude, or vice versa. His manner of behaviour on screen became almost organic. His body movements intuitively found their position like the mirrors of a kaleidoscope find theirs.

Warner

The birth of the myth

James Dean met his death on 30 September 1955, at 17.58 p.m., at the wheel of a silver racing Porsche. He had gone to Salinas to challenge the autumn trophy. The final shots of *Giant* had just been completed (except for a few continuity shots), since Dean's contract stipulated that he was forbidden to take part in any motor race for the duration of the shooting of the film. He had entered for the race by telegram and this race was reputed to be one of the toughest in the USA.

The accident occurred at the intersection of Highway 41 and route 466, at the Grapevine crossing, 19 miles from Paso Robles (eight miles from Salinas), an estate car coming from his left did not give him right of way. The speedometer, which had been recovered from the wreckage, had jammed at 115 mph. James Dean died instantly, his neck having been broken. His mechanic, Rolf Weutherich, was in the passenger seat: photographer Sandford Roth and playboy Bill Hickman were following several miles behind.

After *Giant*, James Dean was on his way to becoming an international superstar, for he was the epitome of the Hollywood ideal which was founded on the principle of the personality achieving perfection. Once dead, it was another James Dean who would eclipse the first: the mythical James Dean. The day after his death, obituaries crowded the pages of the newspapers, the Fairmount News, the local newspaper for Dean's hometown, published a special edition. The publicity department at Warner Bros., which had prepared the release of *Rebel Without A Cause*, and was planning that of *Giant*, was not unfamiliar with this type of operation. Interviews were held with everyone and anyone, from James Dean's father to the head waiter who served him his meals at the *Villa Capri* in Los Angeles.

65

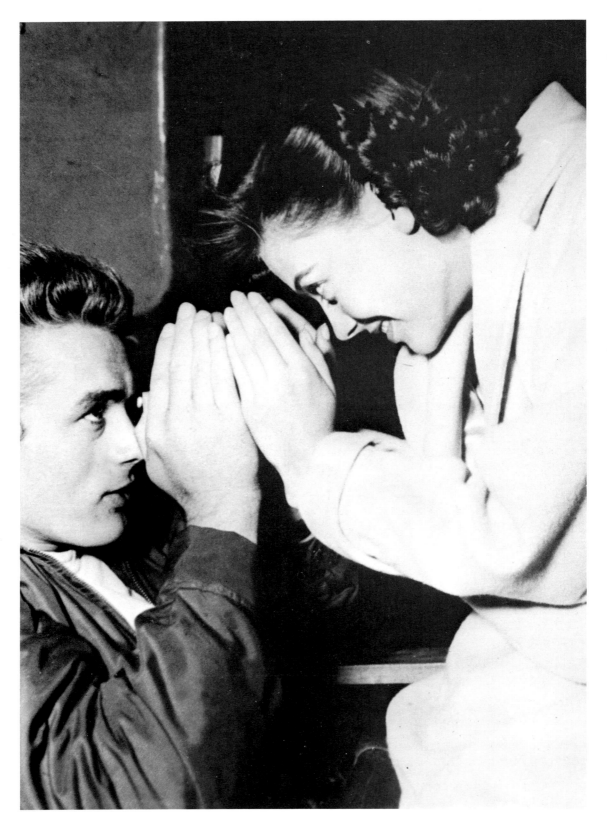

66

Jimmy and Natalie Wood, a true friendship

Jimmy and Anna Maria Pierangeli, a pose for publicity purposes

The myth assumed such proportions that vast sums were to be made by anyone who could lay claim to unpublished photos of Dean.

Following his death, a biography was hastily put together underscoring the points which were most engaging for the reader, finding analogies between the characters he played and his short life, which was underpinned, interpreted and romanticized along the following lines: Once upon a time there was Jimmy, a solitary orphan farmboy. Later on he would always sing 'Nature Boy'. Poor and misunderstood by everybody, he became a film star on the strength of genius alone. He was to have a pure and sublime 'grand amour' with a gentle Madonna, the young Pier Angeli, but her mother thought him to be a rather dubious character and made her daughter marry the more urbane crooner Vic Damone. On their wedding day,

67

Four images of world-weariness

Flight from reality

The passion for glory

The intoxication of speed

68

Death

Jimmy hid close to the church and watched his love leave, hopelessly, he mounted his motorbike and took off at 125 mph. After that nothing mattered any more to Jimmy and nobody could understand his thirst for the absolute. Fools could only mock at the unaffected way in which he took to dressing carelessly: there was nothing surprising either in his killing himself in a noble gesture at 110 mph. It was this image of a neo-romantic archangel struck down by world-weariness, which was distributed to every press agency, and which would be elaborated on to a greater or lesser degree over a period of ten years in every single publication worldwide.

69

70

From stars to idols

At a time when the idolatry of stars was thought to be on the way out, there was an eruption of posthumous interest, the like of which had never been seen before (including the burial of Rudolph Valentino). The idolatry had changed direction and its focus was now the under twenties. When the talkies were born, the Valentino myth had laid bare the secret dreams of women (which since then have tendered that a man need not be handsome). This time it was with the beginnings of cinemascope that the James Dean myth unmasked the transcendant narcissism of youth. James Dean marked the end of an era (that of the great stars) and the beginning of another (that of idols of the young), the character with two faces superimposed on one another which both denigrated and deified him. Over many years the little archangel became a cult and the cult flowered into a sociology, psychoanalysis and enigma, and these became the person of James Dean.

**Romeo and Juliet
1954 version**

**Delicate polishing
of the myth**

Philippe Labro wrote 'Everyone has claimed him for themselves: gays and beatniks, intellectuals and truck drivers, old ladies and girls of fourteen years old, children from the suburbs and young trendies from the 17th arrondissement, New York intellectuals and California sun-worshippers, James Dean belonged to everyone: it would be as well to say that he belonged to no-one.' There is no longer anything surprising in the powerful attraction which he had over young people and it can be explained today with ease. In 1955 the young had no idols, the example of the 'James Dean phenomenon' was a catalyst which was to generate the endless stream of idols to whom young people swore their allegiance. Dean was therefore the one for whom his generation had waited. Apart from the originality of his talent, which was caught up with his time, his outward personality offered the most perfect synthesis of all the physical attributes of adolescence. His sudden death was the basis for the popularization of the myth. We pass silently through the various manifestations of hysteria and fanaticism, whether they be en masse or individual, to which the James

Dean Cult gave rise. The 'facts' emerging from the cult were related unquestioningly almost everywhere.

Claude Bonnevoy wrote:

'The myth reached its peak. It became a religion. As they filed past, people cried on James Dean's grave, as Venus cried on the tomb of Adonis. Three million eight-hundred thousand faithfuls joined clubs set up to celebrate his glory. Over a year after his death Warner Bros. were receiving four thousand letters daily. The sale of his clothes cut up into tiny pieces fetched one dollar per half inch square, the sale of fragments of his car, cut up with a blow lamp after being restored and shown across the country, gatherings at his graveside or in the clubs with music from the films, records, recitals of poetry or songs in his honour, and finally spiritualistic invocations, all for the purpose of reminiscing, combining both Christian devotion to relics and the religious ceremonies of paganism. In the hysterical love for him was the confused quest for a god, embodying both a sun god and a violent god, perhaps the cousin of Dionysus, the figure most often quoted by analysts when discussing the case of James Dean, but one who remains nameless.'

This new Evangelist according to Saint Jimmy was not without irritation for some. Whether it is desirable or not, eternal vestiges of this already ancient religion, such as James Dean's place in the Hollywood Wax Museum, in his costume from *Giant* will always remain among the immortals. A painting signed by Kendall showing him as Hamlet was exhibited on Sunset Boulevard, his bust, also sculpted by Kendall, graces the Hall of Immortals at the University of Princeton. Another monumental bust, which Dean had himself commissioned from the sculptress Peyot Wing, occupies pride of place at Fairmount High School. The James Dean Memorial Foundation was to become a national institution in the same way as the American Legion, and Fairmount town council, with the help of the Governor of Indiana, created 'a society for

the mutual assistance of young people whose physical aspect was closely or remotely redolent of the greatest child genius in the country'!

More prosaic is the life size replica of James Dean's face moulded in 'miracle flesh' (a plastic material which heats up when touched and imitates flesh). One factory sold thousands of these throughout the United States at $40 each. Following this, a Broadway make-up artist took to selling cushions bearing the printed portrait of James Dean and made his fortune in three months.

In 1966, on the occasion of the 11th anniversary of his death, Warner Bros. re-released his three films at selected cinemas only in a number of capital cities, and in association with this, articles about him reappeared causing a James Dean revival. A whole new generation discovered James Dean, albeit with less mysticism that the previous one. Those proselytes displayed a sentimental and nostalgic admiration for him which some people felt for the stars of yesteryear. It is obvious that James Dean will remain an eternally frozen moment of youth. From now on, adolescents will discover themselves in *East of Eden*, dream themselves into *Rebel Without A Cause*, and be troubled by *Giant*, in the same way as people identified with heroes of literature in the past. The spell which he still holds over youth has defied the passage of time, and local cinemas merely have to advertize a screening of his films to ensure that they are sold out for weeks. The poster craze is additional proof of this. Publishers have revealed that the biggest sales of large format posters have been those of James Dean.

James Dean now inclines towards becoming the patron saint of young film actors, and it would have doubtless been preferable if that is all he had been after his death. But, idolatry has its reasons, of which reason knows nothing, thus the taste for the morbid attributed to young people in the James Dean cult is questionable, since the actor's death was experienced more as fiction, and for his fans the legend was merely a fourth film: then there is the rumour, which has always had its believers, making James Dean a disfigured hero hidden in a hospital. There was no need for this popularized resurrection for James Dean to live on, since, as we all know, stars never die and poets only feign death. James Dean is therefore not dead, he can only 'play dead' and we should recognize that this final role by James Byron Dean is one of pure genius.

THE TRILOGY OF
THE UNLOVED ONE

EAST OF EDEN

Kazan prepares to shoot. In his viewfinder Will Hamilton (Albert Dekker),
Adam Trask (Raymond Massey) and James Dean's back

EAST OF EDEN

1917. Salinas Valley, California. Cal Trask (James Dean) drives his father Adam (Raymond Massey), his brother Aron (Richard Davalos) and Aron's fiancée, Abram (Julie Harris) to despair.

Cal discovers his supposedly dead mother, Kate (Jo Van Fleet), runs a house of ill-repute in the town. At a carnival he is tenderly attracted to Abram. As his father is financially ruined, Cal gives him a large sum of money on the occasion of his birthday which he has made from a business deal. Rejected and bruised, he gives full vent to his violent nature and tells his brother of the scandalous existence of their mother. Aron joins the army and goes off to war. Adam suffers a stroke. Cal and Abram are at his bedside. The reconciliation is imminent. Love, in turn, also enters the picture. Cain, after killing Abel, withdraws to east of Eden.

79

Cal Trask (James Dean), his brother Aron (Richard Davalos) and Abram (Julie Harris)

During rehearsals of the balcony scene

82

Between shots, a shave in the cab of an amused mechanic and under the watchful eye of Burl Ives

In the world of John Steinbeck

Raymond Massey, Lonny Chapman, Richard Davalos, Julie Harris, James Dean and Albert Dekker

An enthusiastic send-off for the lettuces

A stranger, his mother Kate (Jo Van Fleet)

87

The psychological tale of the life of a boy of seventeen

A shot off the set

Special shot for the on-set photographer

An out-take

Kate's house is no more than a brothel. Kate and Ann (Lois Smith)

89

Cal enters Kate's boudoir . . .

. . . but is thrown out by a bouncer (Harry Cording)

A scene which might have come from a Jack Kerouac novel▶

95

Sheriff Sam Cooper (Burl Ives) tells Cal how Kate, his mother, had taken a shot at Adam before disappearing

Adam Trask (Raymond Massey) is a hard and strict man. Cal suffers from
never receiving his affection. Raymond Massey, Richard Davalos,
James Dean and Harold Gordon in the role of Mr Albrecht

Cal decides to speculate on beans with Will Hamilton (Albert Dekker)

Richard Davalos, Julie Harris, Harold Gordon, Lois Smith and James Dean Relaxing between shots.

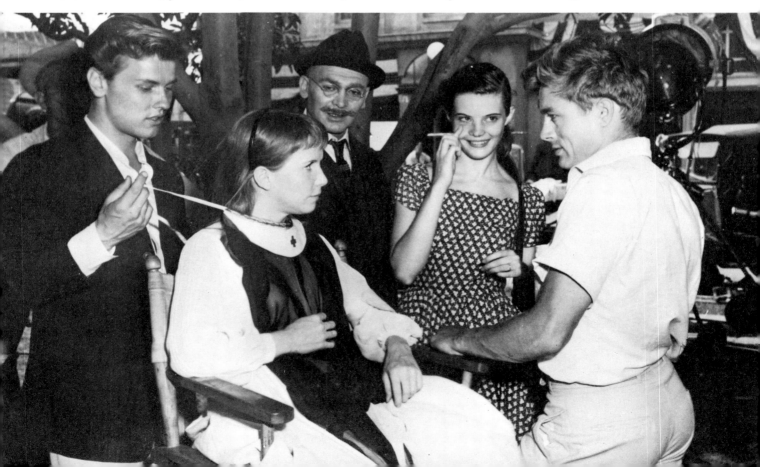

At the fair, Cal and Abram feel attracted to one another

Scenes edited out

Cal flies to the aid of
Aron and Mr Albrecht▶

Three publicity shots, and a still from the film

For his birthday . . .

Cal gives his father the money
which equals love . . .

His father refuses it . . .

Cal takes his brother to the brothel

Abram will save Cal by bringing about a reconciliation with his father

With his director Elia Kazan and three children appearing in the Carnival sequence

While *East of Eden* filled the screen, a new type of music erupted which would kindle the passions of the young, Rock 'n' Roll. Its hero, a previous unknown, was Elvis Presley

2 REBEL WITHOUT A CAUSE

A small provincial middle-class town in the United States. An adolescent, Jim Stark (James Dean) is apprehended one evening in a state of inebriation. At the police station two other adolescents, Judy (Natalie Wood) and Plato (Sal Mineo), have also been arrested. Inspector Ray (Edward Platt), whose job it is to deal with juvenile delinquency, realizes that all three are the victims of domestic problems. Jim suffers from the spineless and cowardly behaviour of his father. Judy, too, has a difficult and unsatisfactory relationship with her estranged father. Plato is the son of a divorced actress, and his parents have always been indifferent towards him.

The following day, Jim, a new arrival at the university, is forced to confront Buzz (Corey Allen), 'the gang leader', in a knife fight, and emerges victorious. However, Buzz demands a new test, and dares him to a 'chicken run', in which he is killed.

Jim feels responsible for the accident which resulted in Buzz's death and asks his parents for advice. In vain. They can show only their disappointment. He then remembers Inspector Ray and decides to go and find him, but he is not there.

Buzz's gang, suspecting that Jim has grassed to the police, sets out to look for him. Jim, Judy and Plato, seek refuge in an abandoned house. Plato in a moment of panic shoots and kills a member of the gang, Moose (Nick Adams). Despite Jim's intervention, Plato is himself shot by a policeman.

Jim and Judy are distraught, but try to forget the whole incident through their love for one another.

The film's opening shot: Jim (James Dean) is slumped drunk on the pavement, where he plays with a clockwork monkey

The 'unloved
one', son of a
weak father (Jim
Backus) and an
authoritarian
mother (Ann
Doran), in
Inspector Ray's
(Edward Platt)
office

James Dean with mother (Ann Doran), grandmother (Virginia Brissac) and father (Jim Backus)

Jimmy, concerned with the *mise en scène*, **listens to a technical consultant**

Jim arrives at Dawson High School

116

Rehearsals before shooting

With a specialist in swordsmanship

Dean puts on a protective vest

A make-up artist simulates a cut

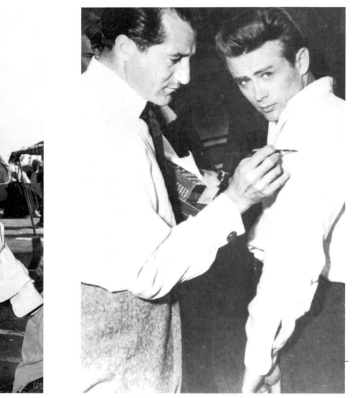

118

. . . Between shots . . .

119

Buzz (Corey Allen) forces the newcomer into combat. Dennis Hopper is recognizable in the role of Goon

**The obsession for self-assertion
and violence 'for the sake of honour'**

The lady wishes her knight 'good luck' before the 'chicken run'

Dennis Hopper (Goon), Natalie Wood (Judy), James Dean
A classic portrayal of tragedy

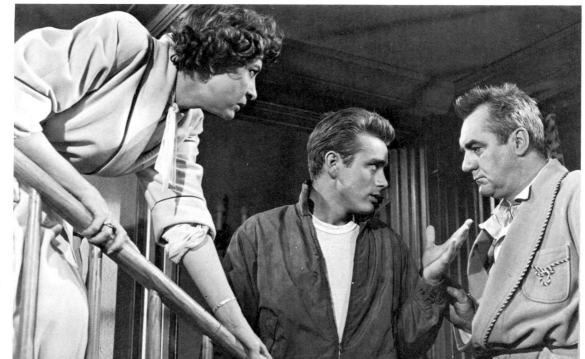

124

The laxity and cowardliness of his father causes Jim to erupt into violence

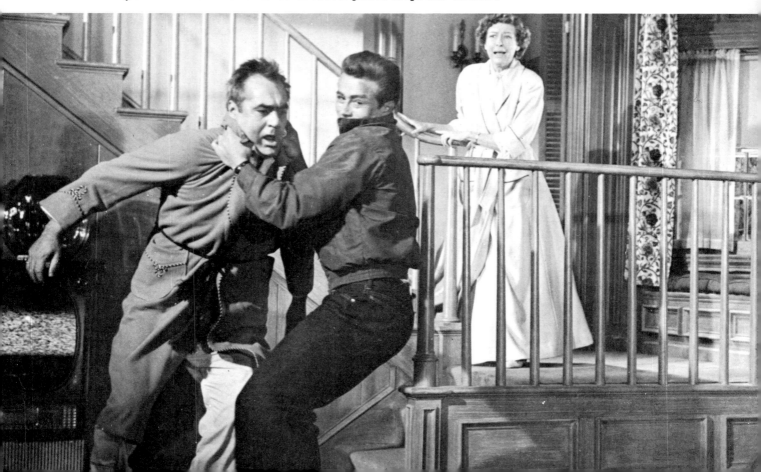

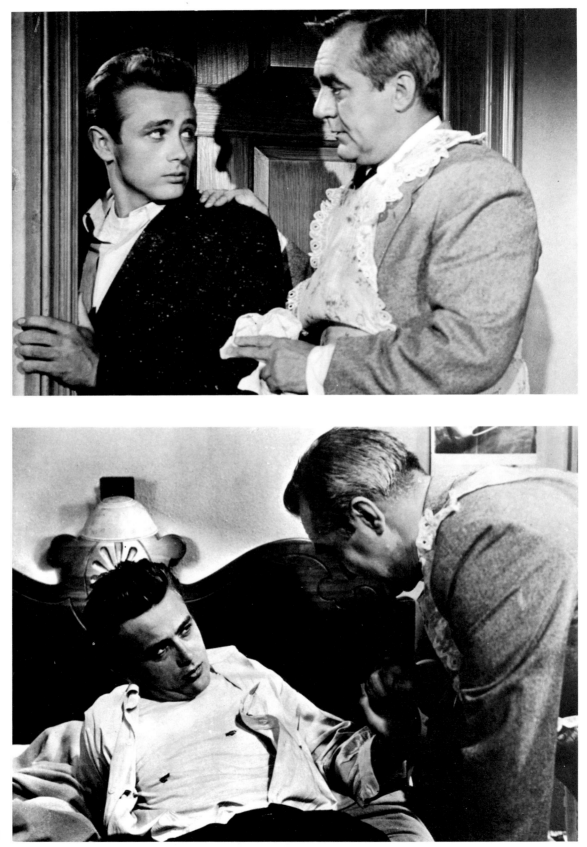

126

**The most modern idyll in
the history of the cinema**

**Jim Stark and Judy adopt
the young Plato (Sal Mineo)**

129

The refuge of an abandoned house

130

131

Where the corridor
diverges, Plato
brandishes a gun and
takes flight. The
police are on his trail.

Jim has unloaded Plato's gun, but the police still shoot him

All they need is love . . .

Bick Benedict (Rock Hudson), a wealthy Texan rancher, returns from Maryland where he had just married Leslie (Elizabeth Taylor). Bick's sister, Luz (Mercedes McCambridge), who runs the ranch, dies suddenly after falling from a horse. In her will she leaves a plot of land to one of her poor cowhands, Jett Rink (James Dean).

Jett Rink, who is secretly in love with Leslie, strikes oil, making him extremely wealthy and thus he is able to compete with the Benedicts, provoking them, and even humiliating them at a grandiose reception which they are giving.

Rink, despite the power which he has acquired, lives a life of solitude. He will never have Leslie's love and will end up a drunkard.

Luz (Mercedes McCambridge) is the undisputed head of the Benedict clan

Unspoken love for Leslie (Elizabeth Taylor)

One of the few intimate scenes in *Giant* where Dean is able to excel

142

But Jett Rink has found oil on his land . . .
The poor cowhand will become cynical and
unyielding

Black gold . . . equals prosperity

146

Oil . . . a heaven-sent gift for Jett Rink

Sprayed with oil for the scene. An assistant wipes his eyes for him

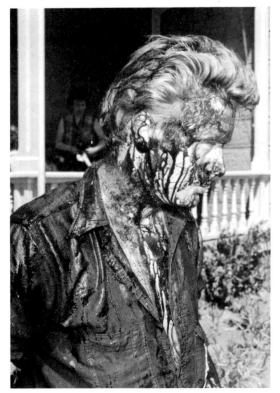

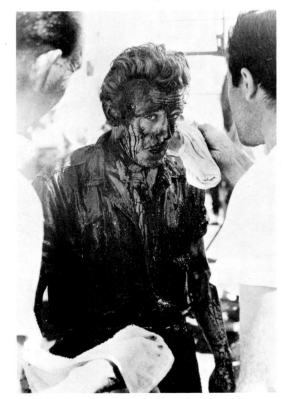

Jett Rink is now the
Benedicts' rival. Rock
Hudson (left) and
Elizabeth Taylor (right)

153

Years later. With Luz Benedict II (Carroll Baker)

The megalomania of the Texan oil barons

Luz Benedict II

One of the wardrobe
tests for James Dean as
the fifty-year-old Jett
Rink

Publicity shots

158

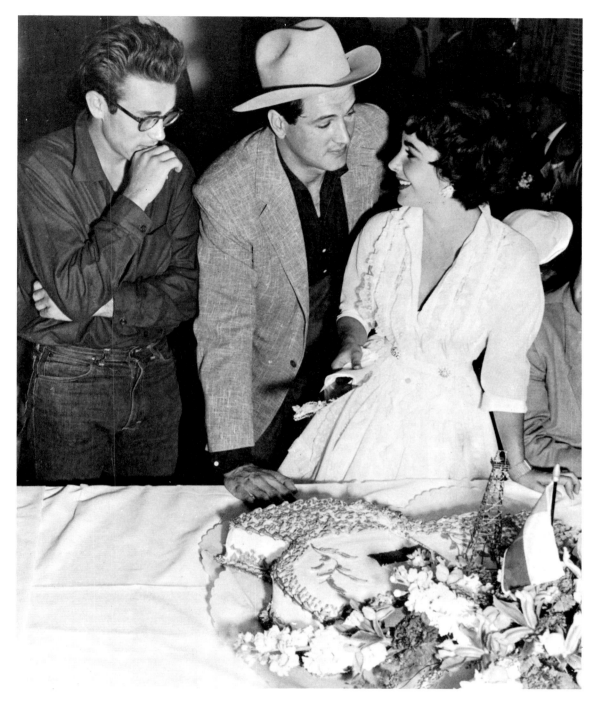

Happy endings. James Dean, Rock Hudson and Elizabeth Taylor slice into the cake of the last derrick

During shooting, he trained with the lasso every day

'He was the child who goes to a secret corner and refuses to speak' (Nicholas Ray)

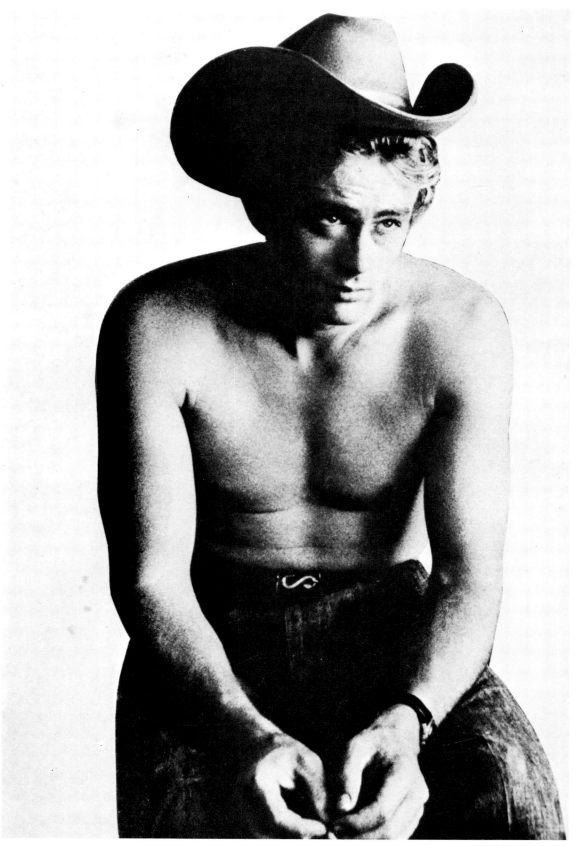

163

164 New York, Times Square, the winter of 1952. This photo was an existentialist inspiration and became the emblem of the 'beat generation'

THE JAMES DEAN STORY

A documentary film, produced by George W. George and Robert Altman, tracing the life and career of James Dean using photographs, clips from his films, and interviews with people with whom he lived and worked.

An out-take from *East of Eden*. In the background Aron (Richard Davalos)

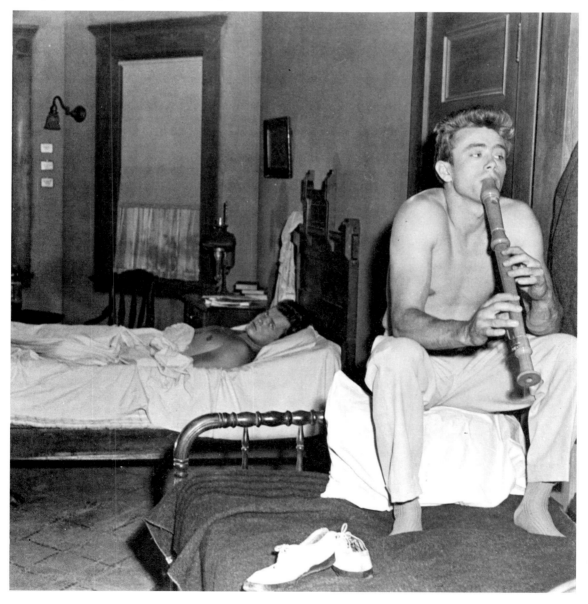

James Dean introduces his young cousin to racing cars, which are his passion

With Natalie Wood and a friend

With Anna Maria Pierangeli scheduled to star with him in *Somebody Up There Likes Me*

In evening dress to accompany Terry Moore to the premiere of *Sabrina*

167

James Dean and Pierangeli tackling their scripts for *Somebody Up There Likes Me*

Showing off the award given to him by the readers of the French magazine, *Cinémonde*▶

**Receiving instructions from his director for a
tricky sequence in *Rebel Without A Cause***

Two emperors of derision

To play the role of Jett, Jimmy wanted to know everything about Texan life. Here he is seen learning about country & western

171

Camaraderie

◀**Friendship: Nicholas Ray**

**His passion: Dean driving
an Austin Healey**

Forever speed. The Porsche which he will drive in his first race

Fate: the morning of 30 September 1955.
Within a few minutes . . .

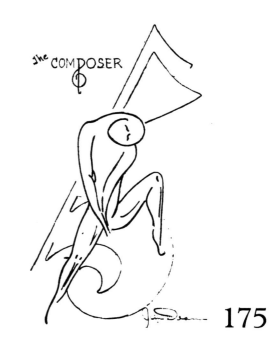

the COMPOSER

Drawing by James Dean, 'Treble clef'

175

At Fairmount cemetery, Jimmy collects his thoughts by the grave of one of his uncles whose forename was one of predestination: Cal, that of the character he played in *East of Eden*. This same cemetery was his final resting place

If spring were to pass too quickly,
Would it be the fault of a bird?
                    (Chanson de Corée)

HOBBIES

Hobbies

This sculpture, often attributed to James Dean, is in fact the work of an artist wanting to express the poignant image of his despair of life

He was an excellent photographer. D. Dalton said that, 'His angles are always remarkable, they could be by Cocteau.'

He took some very good portrait shots of Pierangeli

179

Perfect muleta technique

At Eartha Kitt's ballet class

180

On the Palm Springs circuit

The pleasure of the motorbike

181

THE FACES OF
A GENERATION

Alain Delon, *Is Paris burning?*

Influences . . .

184 **Paul Newman who took the James Dean part in** *Somebody Up There Likes Me*, **directed by Robert Wise**

Gérard Philipe, the post-war incarnation of youth 185

... Montgomery Clift

. . . Gérard Blain in France

. . . Horst Buchholz in Germany

. . . A young Italian actor

186

. . .Zbigniev Cybulski in Poland　　　. . . Johnny Halliday

James Dean lookalikes turned up all over the world. Here is a young British actor

But the myth wasn't confined to men only:
This was the era of MM and BB

Marilyn Monroe and Brigitte Bardot also made their indelible mark

189

James Dean lives on . . .

191

James Dean . . .

192

Television in 1953. Rehearsal for the play *The Thief*

James Dean . . .

James Dean . . .

The reflection of a generation of Americans in the eyes of one youth

196

A radiant and sharp image, as if in defiance of the laws of death,
an image which nothing can erase.
One is reminded of Cocteau when he spoke of Rimbaud:
'He has gone . . . but he will return . . .'

199

200

FILMOGRAPHY

FIXED BAYONETS – 1951

Director: Sam Fuller. **Cast:** Richard Basehart, Gene Evans. **Production:** 20th Century Fox.

'James Dean played the frightened G.I. who, at the end of the film, announces that Richard Basehart and the other survivors will cross the river. (Samuel Fuller. *Présence du Cinéma*, No. 20).

SAILOR BEWARE – 1951

Director: Hall Walker. **Cast:** Dean Martin, Jerry Lewis. **Production:** Paramount.

Towards the second third of the film, Jerry Lewis takes part in a boxing match, James Dean is the second for Lewis' opponent (a few words of dialogue).

HAS ANYBODY SEEN MY GAL – 1952

Director: Douglas Sirk. **Cast:** Charles Coburn, Rock Hudson. **Production:** Universal.

James Dean enters a drugstore and orders an ice cream from Charles Coburn. The scene recurs throughout the film.

EAST OF EDEN – 1954

Director: Elia Kazan. **Screenplay:** Paul Osborn, from the final episode of John Steinbeck's novel. **Dialogue:** Guy Thomajan. **Camerawork:** Ted McCord (Cinemascope, Warnercolor). **Music:** Leonard Rosenman. **Sets:** George James Hopkins, James Basevi and Malcolm Bert. **Editing:** Owen Marks. **Costumes:** Anna Hill Johnstone. **Assistant producers:** Don Page, Horace Hough. **Technical adviser:** John Hambleton. **Production:** Elia Kazan, Warner Bros. **Length:** 115 mins. **Release:** U.S.A., 9 April 1955.

Cast: Julie Harris (Abram), James Dean (Cal Trask), Raymond Massey (Adam Trask), Richard Davalos (Aron Trask), Jo Van Fleet (Kate), Burl Ives (Sheriff Sam Cooper), Albert Dekker (Will Hamilton), Lois Smith (Ann), Harold Gordon (Mr Albrecht), Timothy Carey (Joe), Mario Siletti (Piscora), Lonny Chapman (Roy), Nick Dennis (Rantany).

REBEL WITHOUT A CAUSE – 1955

Director: Nicholas Ray. **Screenplay:** Stewart Stern, from Irving Shulman's adaptation of an original idea by Nicholas Ray. **Camerawork:** Ernest Haller (Cinemascope, Warnercolor). **Music:** Leonard Rosenman. **Editing:** William Ziegler. **Sets:** William Wallace. **Artistic direction:** Malcolm Bert. **Sound:** Stanley Jones. **Production:** David Weisbart, Warner Bros. **Length:** 111 mins. **Shooting:** 9 weeks. **Release:** U.S.A., 29 October 1955.

Cast: James Dean (Jim Stark), Natalie Wood (Judy), Jim Backus (Jim's father), Ann Doran (Jim's mother), William Hopper (Judy's father), Rochelle Hudson (Judy's mother), Virginia Brissac (Jim's grandmother), Sal Mineo (Plato), Corey Allen (Buzz), Dennis Hopper (Goon), Edward Platt (Inspector Ray), Marietta Canty (Plato's nanny), Beverly Long (Helen), Robert Foulk (Inspector Gene), Frank Mazzola (Crunch), Jack Simmons (Cookie), Nick Adams (Moose), Ian Wolfe (lecturer), Dick Wassel (guide), Jack Grinnage, Tom Bernard, Cliff Morris, Steffi Sidney (members of the gang).

201

GIANT – 1965

Director: George Stevens. **Screenplay:** Fred Guiol and Ivan Moffat, from Edna Ferber's novel. **Dialogue:** Henry Ginsberg. **Camerawork:** William C. Mellor (Warnercolor). **Music** composed and conducted by: Dimitri Tiomkin. **Sets:** Ralph Hurst.

Editing: William Horning, assisted by Fred Bohaman and Phil Anderson. **Costumes:** Marjorie Best and Moss Mabry. **Sound:** Earl Crain. **Assistant producer:** Joe Rickards, Fred Guiol, Russ Llewellyn. **Assistant cameraman:** Edwin DuPar. **Technical adviser:** Bob Hinckle. **Director of production:** Tom Andre. **Executive Producer:** Boris Ceven. **Producers:** George Stevens and Henry Ginsberg (Warner Bros.). **Length:** 200 mins. **Shooting commenced:** June 1955. **Release:** U.S.A., 24 November 1956.

Cast: James Dean (Jett Rink), Elizabeth Taylor (Leslie Benedict), Rock Hudson (Bick Benedict), Jane Withers (Vashti Snythe), Chill Wills (Uncle Bawley), Mercedes McCambridge (Luz Benedict), Carroll Baker (Luz Benedict II), Dennis Hopper (Jordan Benedict III), Judith Evelyn (Mrs Horace Lynnton), Robert Taylor (Sir David Karfrey), Earl Holliman (Bob Dace), Robert Nichols (Pinky Snythe), Alexander Scourby (Old Polo), Sal Mineo (Angel Obregon III), Fran Bennett (Judy Benedict), Charles Watts (Whiteside), Elsa Cardenas (Juana), Carolyn Craig (Lacey Lynnton), Monte Halo (Bale Clinch), Mary Ann Edwards (Adarene Clinch), Sheb Woolley (Gabe Targot), Victor Millan (Angel Obregon I), Mickey Simpson (Sarge), Pilar Del Rey (Mrs Obregon), Maurice Jara (Iona Lano), Napoleon Whiting (Swazey), Tim Menard (Lupe), Ray Whiting (Watts).

202

THE JAMES DEAN STORY – 1957

Director: Louis Clyde Stoumen. **Written** by Stewart Stern. **Narrated** by Martin Gabel. **Music** composed and conducted by Leith Stevens (Song by Jay Livingston and Ray Evans, sung by Tommy Sand). **Production:** George W. George and Robert Altman. **Length:** 82 mins. **Distribution:** Warner Bros.

A documentary film tracing the life and career of James Dean using photographs, film clips and interviews with people with whom he lived and worked. The sequences concerned with the accident are narrated by Nelson, the road safety officer who headed the enquiry. A percentage of the box office takings from the film were donated to the James Dean Memorial Foundation, in Fairmount.

JAMES DEAN
The first American teenager – 1975

Director: Ray Connolly. **Production:** David Puttnam and Sandy Lieberson (V.P.S. Ltd). **Narrated** by Stacey Keach. **Music:** David Bowie, Elton John and The Eagles.

JAMES DEAN – 1976

T.V. film by Robert Butler. Cast: Stephen McHattie in the role of James Dean and Michael Brando as William Bast. Portrayal of the friendship between producer William Bast and James Dean and the actor's love life with Christine White and the dancer Dizzy Sheridan. **Music:** Billy Goldenberg.

COME BACK TO THE FIVE AND DIME, JIMMY DEAN, JIMMY DEAN – 1982

Director: Robert Altman. **Production:** Viacom Enterprises.

BIBLIOGRAPHY

BOOKS ON JAMES DEAN

James Dean: A biography, by William Bast, 153pp, Ballantine Books, New York, 1956.

I, James Dean, by T.T. Thomas, 128pp, illustrated, Popular Library, New York, 1957.

James Dean ou le mal de vivre, by Yves Salgues, 220pp, illustrated, Éditions Pierre Horay, Paris, 1957.

James Dean et notre Jeunesse, by Xavier Grall, Éditions du Cerf, Paris, 1958.

Rebel, by Royston Ellis (novel about James Dean), illustrated, Consul Books, London, 1965.

James Dean, A Short Life, by Venable Herndon, Doubeday and Co., 1974.

James Dean Story, Édition René Chateau, 1975.

The Real James Dean, by John Gilmore, Pyramid Books, New York, 1975.

James Dean, The Mutant King, W.H. Allen, London, 1975.

James Dean, by John Howlett, Plexus Publishing, London, 1975.

The Films of James Dean, by Mark Whitman (General Editor: Susan d'Arcy, Great Britain, 1974, reprinted in 1975 and 1977).

James Dean Rebell und Idol, by Michael Marks, Series 'Von Fans für Fans', No. 2 (Produced by Claude Berck, Munich, 1977).

James Dean, by Von Horst Königstein, Dressler Verlag, Hamburg, 1977.

James Dean Revisited, text and photographs, by Dennis Stock, Penguin Books, 1978.

James Dean, Rebell, Idol, Legend. Verlay GmbH, Hamburg, 1981.

James Dean, by Jean-Loup Bourget, Édition Henry Veyrier, 1983.

James Dean, American Icon, by David Dalton and Ron Cayen, Sidgwick & Jackson, 1984.

James Dean, by Sanford Roth and Benlah Roth, Bahia Verlag, Munich, 1984.

La Malédiction des Stars, by Henry Chapier, contains an important chapter on the James Dean 'phenomenon'. Édition Michel Laffont-Carrère, 1985.

BOOKS AND REVIEWS DEVOTED IN PART TO JAMES DEAN

Books

De Tom à James Dean, by Raymond de Becker, Chapter 7, 'James Dean ou la quête d'un dieu du printemps', 30pp, Éditions Fayard, 1959.

Les Stars, by Edgar Morin, 14pp illustrated on 'The case of James Dean', Éditions du Seuil, Paris, May 1957.

Fabulous Yesterday, by Lewis Gillenson, 246pp, New York, 1961.

Hollywood in Transition, by Mac Cann and Richard Dyer, 208pp, Boston, 1962.

Here Today, by Louise Tanner, 320pp, (21 pages are concerned with James Dean), New York, 1963.

The Popular Arts, by Stuart Hall and Paddy Whannel, 480pp, illustrated, New York, 1965.

Reviews:

Marie Claire, No. 25, November 1956.

Paris-Match, March 1957.

La Méthode (Actors' Studio special), No. 2, January 1961.

Salut les Copains, Nos. 5, 6, 7, 15 (abridged and revised text of Yves Salgues book, *James Dean ou le mal de vivre,* illustrated with a number of unpublished photos).

Film Fame, edited by Warren Goldsmith, 210pp, illustrated, Beverly Hills, 1966.

Screen Fact, No. 8 (James Dean, by G. Ringgold).

Daily Variety (23rd Anniversary Issue).

James Dean, by Nicholas Ray, illustrated, 1956.

ALBUMS AND SPECIAL EDITIONS DEVOTED ENTIRELY TO JAMES DEAN

Official James Dean Anniversary Book, 76pp, 100 photos, Dell Publishing Co., New York, 1956.

James Dean Album, 68pp, 175 photos, Ideal Publishing Co., New York, 1956.

The Real James Dean Story, Fawcett Publications, 1956.

James Dean Returns (Full story of Judy Collins' search for James Dean), 66pp, illustrated, Rave Publishing Co., New York, 1956.

The Late James Dean, Fans' Star Library, No. 16 of 16 March 1959, London.

Screen Legends, James Dean (His life and his legend), by Gene Ringgold, 32pp, illustrated, May 1965.

FILM REPORTS

East of Eden: *Mon Film* (No. 474, September 1955). *Ciné-monde* (No. 1520, 24 September 1963), *Star-Ciné-Roman* (No. 152, 1st April 1963).

Rebel Without A Cause: *Mon Film* (No. 510, 30th May 1956), *Ciné-Revue* (No. 2, 13th January 1956). *Cinémonde* (No. 1124, 23rd February, 1956). *Cinémonde* (No. 1475, 13th November 1962). *Star-Ciné-Roman* (No. 151, 15th March 1963).

Giant: *Ciné-Revue* (No. 49, 7th December 1956). *Star-Ciné-Roman* (No. 153, 15th April 1963).

The James Dean Story: *Ciné-Revue* (No. 27, 5th July 1957).

FILM REVIEWS

East of Eden: by P. Clairac (Ciné-Revue, No. 16, Cannes Film Festival Special, 22nd April 1965); François Truffaut (Arts, 26th October 1955); Jean de Baroncelli (Le Monde, 31st October 1955); Pierre Leprophon (Cette Semaine, 1st November 1955); André Bazin (L'Observateur, 3rd November 1955), François Truffaut (Cahiers du Cinéma, No. 56, February 1956, and in Cinémonde, No. 1108, 3rd November 1955 and No. 1128, 22nd March 1956).

Rebel Without A Cause: Henri Magnan (Les Lettres Françaises, 5th April 1956); Eric Rohmer (Cahiers du Cinéma, No. 56, May 1956); Charles Chaboud (Cinéma 56, No. 11, May 1956); Roger Tailleur (Positif, No. 17, June/July 1956).

Giant: Louis Marcorelles (Cahiers du Cinéma, No. 67, January 1957); Georges Sadoul (Les Lettres Françaises, 21st March 1957); Jean-François Held (Ciné-Révélations, 21st march 1957); Ado Kyrou (Positif, No. 23, April 1957); Eric Rohmer (Cahiers du Cinéma, No. 70, April 1957); Louis Sequin (Positif, No. 24, May 1957 and in Cinémonde, No. 1180, 21st March 1957).

The James Dean Story: Jacques Siclier (Radio-Télé-Cinéma, No. 460, 9th November 1958).

205

DISCOGRAPHY

East of Eden: music from the film, conducted by Art Mooney (45rpm, MGM 123.12 – side 1 of the record). By Victor young (45rpm Decca). By the Buddy Bregman Orchestra (45 rpm E.R.A.). By the Eric Jupp Orchestra (45 rpm. Columbia D.B. 3817).

Rebel Without A Cause: music from the film, conducted by Art Mooney (45 rpm. MGM 123.12 – side 2 of the record).

Giant: original soundtrack of the film, conducted by Art Mooney (LP. Capitol W-773- French edition LP – E.A.P. 1.779).

'Themes from the three films of James Dean': by the Dick Jacobs Orchestra and the George Cates Orchestra (45rpm. Coral F.C.V. 18066).

East of Eden and **Rebel Without A Cause:** themes of both films, conducted by Leonard Rosenman, side 2 from the original soundtrack of the film **The Chapman Report** (LP. WB 1478).

The James Dean Story: music from the film, conducted by Chet Baker (LP. World 2005 and World Pacific L/D 369.30, French edition distributed by Vogue).

The James Dean Story: original film soundtrack (LP. Capitol W-881).

A Tribute to James Dean: by Art Mooney (LP. MGM 923 and LP. London Records MHP 2040, British edition).

James Dean plays Conga drums: 45 rpm. Romeo (a tape recording found after his death).

The Ballad of James Dean: sung by Dylan Todd (45rpm. RCA – FA 6463).

James Dean Album: 45 rpm. TNT No. 1 E.P. (two discs exploiting the cult).

A Tribute to James Dean: music from *Giant* by Ray Haindorf and his orchestra, and soundtrack of *East of Eden* and *Rebel Without A Cause* (Columbia ACL 940).

James Dean: original soundtrack dialogue and music from James Dean's three greatest performances (Warner Bros. K 56122, 1975).

Leonard Rosenman conducts music from the films of James Dean (Sunset Records, London 1978).

Songs of the James Dean Era: Gene Vincent (EMI, made in Italy).

PHOTO
JAMES DEAN MISCELLANY

Lecture: 'James Dean ou le mythe de l'adolescence dans le cinéma contemporain', by Jacques Siclier, given at the Sociétés Savantes, Paris, on 26th March 1957. (The lecture was partly improvised.) An extract was published in the Bulletin du Ciné-Club Universitaire, No. 16, 4th April 1957).

Radio Broadcasts: A programme by Roger Briard, on James Dean, with the man who dubbed James Dean's voice in French, Michel François (broadcast on 27th May 1959, at 8.00 p.m. by Paris-Inter).

Television Broadcasts: Perspectives sur James Dean (broadcast 3rd August 1968, at 9.40 p.m.) This programme was a forty minute extract from the Robert Altman film, *The James Dean Story*, with a commentary by Martine Ferrière.

La légende du siècle: James Dean, programme by Claude Santelli, made by Monique Chapelle (broadcast on 1st January 1969, at 5.40 p.m., on the 1st channel. Length: 40 mins). By interviewing young people, the programme attempts to show problems confronting modern youth. What did James Dean mean to them, in 1968?.

Le Théâtre Vidéo Lux: interview for the screening of *East of Eden*, 1955.

Steve Allen Show: a homage to James Dean, 1956.

Colgate Variety Hour: a prize awarded posthumously by Modern Screen for James Dean's twenty-fifth birthday.

The James Dean Legend: a homage to James Dean on CBS, produced by Associated Rediffusion (GB) 1957.

French television broadcast James Dean's three films in 1979 and 1981 and for the third time, *Rebel Without A Cause* on TF1 on 30th June 1985 in the French version.

207